W9-CHI-496

FIRST SCIENCE

Motion

by Kay Manolis

Consultant:
Duane Quam, M.S. Physics
Chair, Minnesota State
Academic Science Standards
Writing Committee

BELLWETHER MEDIA • MINNEAPOLIS, MN

Note to Librarians, Teachers, and Parents:

Blastoff! Readers are carefully developed by literacy experts and combine standards-based content with developmentally appropriate text.

Level 1 provides the most support through repetition of high-frequency words, light text, predictable sentence patterns, and strong visual support.

Level 2 offers early readers a bit more challenge through varied simple sentences, increased text load, and less repetition of high-frequency words.

Level 3 advances early-fluent readers toward fluency through increased text and concept load, less reliance on visuals, longer sentences, and more literary language.

Level 4 builds reading stamina by providing more text per page, increased use of punctuation, greater variation in sentence patterns, and increasingly challenging vocabulary.

Level 5 encourages children to move from "learning to read" to "reading to learn" by providing even more text, varied writing styles, and less familiar topics.

Whichever book is right for your reader, Blastoff! Readers are the perfect books to build confidence and encourage a love of reading that will last a lifetime!

This edition first published in 2009 by Bellwether Media.

No part of this publication may be reproduced in whole or in part without written permission of the publisher. For information regarding permission, write to Bellwether Media Inc., Attention: Permissions Department, Post Office Box 19349, Minneapolis, MN 55419.

Library of Congress Cataloging-in-Publication Data
Manolis, Kay.
  Motion / by Kay Manolis.
    p. cm. — (Blastoff! readers. First science)
  Includes bibliographical references and index.
  Summary: "Simple text and full color photographs introduce beginning readers to motion. Developed by literacy experts for students in kindergarten through third grade"–Provided by publisher.
  ISBN-13: 978-1-60014-225-3 (hardcover : alk. paper)
  ISBN-10: 1-60014-225-7 (hardcover : alk. paper)
  1. Motion–Juvenile literature. 2. Friction–Juvenile literature. 3. Force and energy–Juvenile literature. I. Title.

  QC133.5.M36 2009
  531'.11–dc22   2008021304

Contents

What Is Motion?

A throw sends a ball soaring. It may fly all the way across the field. The ball is in motion. Motion is the act of going from one place or **position** to another.

There is motion all around you. Cars move on the street. People and animals walk, run, and play. Machines move as they do work. A clock's hands move as time passes.

Speed

Everything that moves has a **speed**. This is a measure of how fast or slow something moves from one place to another in a certain amount of time.

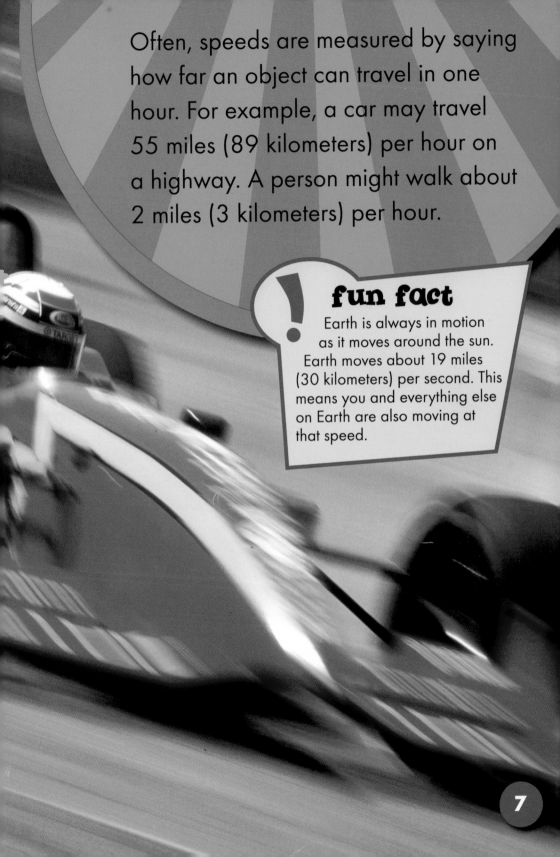

Often, speeds are measured by saying how far an object can travel in one hour. For example, a car may travel 55 miles (89 kilometers) per hour on a highway. A person might walk about 2 miles (3 kilometers) per hour.

fun fact

Earth is always in motion as it moves around the sun. Earth moves about 19 miles (30 kilometers) per second. This means you and everything else on Earth are also moving at that speed.

Some motion is extremely fast. This bullet train is one of the fastest land vehicles on Earth. It can move 361 miles (581 kilometers) per hour.

Some motion is much slower. Rivers of snow and ice called **glaciers** move very slowly across land. Many glaciers move just a few inches a day.

Laws of Motion

All motion follows certain rules. These rules are called **laws of motion**. One of these laws says that nothing starts moving by itself. Everything needs a **force** to get it started. A force is a push or a pull. For example, the force of a kick pushes a ball. The force of the wind pushes the blades of a windmill.

fun fact

Sir Isaac Newton was a famous scientist who lived in the 1600s. He was the first person to explain the laws of motion. Scientists today still study Newton's explanations to help them understand how motion works.

Light objects may start moving with only a small amount of force. A small push sends this go-kart moving.

Heavier objects need much greater force to start moving. It takes the force of several people to get this Indy car moving when its engine does not work.

A force can change the direction of a moving object. Say a soccer player kicks a ball toward another team. A person on the other team kicks it back. The force of the second kick changes the ball's direction.

Friction

fun fact

Air and water create friction that slows down moving objects. Airplanes, boats, birds, and many ocean animals have special shapes and smooth surfaces that reduce friction.

Moving objects would keep going forever if no other force acted upon them. When you give your scooter a push, what slows it down? It's a force called **friction**. Friction slows down moving objects and brings them to a stop. Friction happens when any material rubs against another material. Your scooter's tires rub against the sidewalk. This creates friction that slows you down. That is why you have to keep pushing your scooter along.

Action and Reaction

Every force creates another force that pushes back in the opposite direction. This is sometimes called the law of action and reaction.

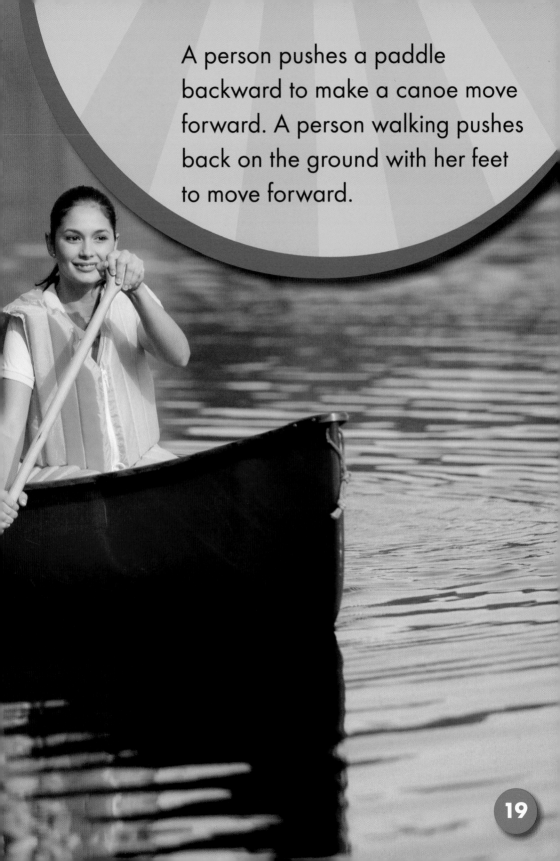

A person pushes a paddle backward to make a canoe move forward. A person walking pushes back on the ground with her feet to move forward.

19

A rocket taking off shows the law of action and reaction. Rocket engines create huge blasts of fire. These push downward to make the rocket move upward. This force pushes the shuttle into space.

Scientists needed to understand the laws of motion to build this amazing vehicle.

Glossary

force—a push or pull; force can cause an object to start, stop, or change the direction of its movement.

friction—a force caused when two surfaces rub together; friction slows down or stops moving objects.

glaciers—rivers of flowing ice and snow

laws of motion—rules that describe how all motions always work; Sir Isaac Newton first explained the laws of motion in the year 1665.

position—the way in which things are placed or arranged

speed—the rate at which an object moves from one place to another

To Learn More

AT THE LIBRARY

Bradley, Kimberly Brubaker. *Forces Make Things Move*. New York: HarperCollins, 2005.

Hewitt, Sally. *Amazing Forces and Movement*. New York: Crabtree, 2008.

Murphy, Bryan. *Experiment with Movement*. Princeton, NJ: Two-Can Publishing, 2001.

ON THE WEB

Learning more about motion is as easy as 1, 2, 3.

1. Go to www.factsurfer.com

2. Enter "motion" into search box.

3. Click the "Surf" button and you will see a list of related web sites.

With factsurfer.com, finding more information is just a click away.

Index